Financial Crimes Enforcement Network

FinCEN BSA Direct Retrieval and Sharing Assessment Report

FINAL

July 10, 2006

Table of Contents

1.0   Executive Summary

The Financial Crimes Enforcement Network (FinCEN) has statutory responsibility as administrator of the Bank Secrecy Act (BSA), and under multiple sections of the USA PATRIOT Act[1], to safeguard the financial system from the abuses of financial crime, including terrorist financing, money laundering, and other illicit activities. To fulfill its mission, FinCEN relies heavily on the use of BSA data, its primary and most important information asset. Over 14 million BSA forms or "reports" are filed by more than 200,000 financial institutions and money services businesses each year. FinCEN shares BSA data with law enforcement and regulatory entities, which rely heavily on its use in enforcement and compliance actions. The demonstrated value of BSA data generated by these filings impels FinCEN to properly manage and extract value from it, and find better and more effective ways to use it. The essential focus of the BSA Direct Retrieval and Sharing (BSA Direct R&S) system, a project conceived of in 2003, is the enhancement of the value and use of BSA data with the aim of helping FinCEN meet these strategic technology goals and support its mission priorities.

In July 2004, FinCEN launched BSA Direct R&S, a data warehouse and information retrieval system, under a contract with Electronic Data Systems (EDS) Corporation (hereinafter referred to as "the Contractor"). BSA Direct R&S is a component of BSA Direct, an umbrella project with several components including retrieval and sharing, electronic filing, and secure access. The electronic filing and secure access components have been operational for a number of years.

BSA Direct R&S has repeatedly missed program milestones and performance objectives. Moreover, the project is significantly over the projected budget. The original cost estimate of $8.9 million for the prime contract increased to $15.1 million. Of that amount, $14.4 million is spent. Estimates indicate that an additional $8 million would be needed before the system could be completed and utilized, and at least $2.5 million more for Operations and Maintenance (O&M) would be required. Given the information contained in this report, even an additional investment of this magnitude would not ensure that FinCEN would achieve the desired product in BSA Direct R&S.

In March 2006, the newly appointed FinCEN Director decided that a stop-work order should be issued in accordance with the relevant contract clause. This action was based on briefings with staff, as well as representatives from MITRE Corporation, the project's Independent Verification and Validation (IV&V) contractor, all of whom identified major project deficiencies. FinCEN's Director determined that an assessment was warranted to evaluate the future viability of the system. Immediately thereafter, a team of FinCEN staff with support from SiloSmashers, a technology-consulting firm, began an assessment of BSA Direct R&S. In addition, FinCEN also contracted with i2S, Inc. to perform an independent technical assessment. The results of both assessments validate the stop-work decision.

The key findings of the FinCEN assessment team (referred to as the "Assessment Team") are as follows:

---

[1] Uniting and Strengthening America by Providing Appropriate Tools Required to Intercept and Obstruct Terrorism (USA PATRIOT) Act of 2001, Pub. L. No. 107-56 (codified in various sections of the United States Code).

- At present, BSA Direct R&S is a partially built system, which integrates a number of best-in-class products that do not function well together.

- The system, as currently configured, cannot be provided to any of FinCEN's users.

- The level of effort and costs to complete the project requirements, address all remaining defects, and operate and maintain the system are likely to be much greater than originally projected.

- Currently, neither FinCEN, nor the contractor or external consultants can definitively predict how close the system is to meeting the requirements or the time, resources, and risks involved in completing the system.

A multitude of problems contributed to the current situation. These include, but are not limited to the following:

- Overly aggressive schedule

- Significant increase in overall project cost

- Unclear project scope and requirements

- Inadequate project governance

- Lack of demonstrated project management expertise by the contractor and FinCEN

- Issues and delays in fully staffing the project by the contractor and FinCEN

- Underestimation of the time and complexity required for Commercial Off-the-Shelf (COTS) integration; and

- Unacceptable system quality

The Assessment Team detailed its findings in this paper and in the accompanying BSA Direct R&S Technical System Assessment. Based on these findings, the team considered the following three options for actions going forward:

Option 1 - Continue the current contract with the contractor, but renegotiate certain terms and conditions.

Option 2 - Terminate the contract and award a new contract to a new company using the existing partially built system as Government furnished equipment.

Option 3 - Terminate the contract with the contractor, assess needs and plan for new capabilities.

Based on FinCEN's strategic mission, as well as the costs, benefits, and risks associated with the three options, the Assessment Team recommends that FinCEN terminate the existing contract, and assess needs and plan for new capabilities. The steps necessary to implement this option include:

- Formalizing a re-planning effort for BSA Direct R&S, to include strategic, technical, and resource planning issues, as well as stakeholder analysis;

- Continuing efforts with the Internal Revenue Service (IRS) to implement WebCBRS as an immediate means of meeting internal and customer needs for BSA data query and analysis tools;

- Evaluating the discrete elements of BSA Direct R&S for salvageability; and

- Developing a roadmap to achieve BSA Direct R&S in steps, as a program with multiple projects, both business and technology-oriented.

2.0   Introduction

FinCEN is the United States' Financial Intelligence Unit (FIU) and is responsible for managing, analyzing, safeguarding, and appropriately sharing financial transaction information collected under the BSA and other authorities.

BSA data represents FinCEN's primary information asset with over 14 million BSA reports filed each year by more than 200,000 U.S. financial institutions. FinCEN shares BSA information with a wide range of customers involved in combating financial crime, including financial regulators, federal, state, and local law enforcement agencies, as well as intelligence agencies and foreign FIUs.

Under Section 361 of the USA PATRIOT Act, FinCEN must establish and "maintain a government-wide data access service, with access to ... information collected by the Department of the Treasury, including report information ...(such as reports on cash transactions, foreign financial agency transactions and relationships, foreign currency transactions, exporting and importing monetary instruments, and suspicious activities)."[2] The BSA Direct R&S vision is to gain constructive control of BSA data processes, improve the data quality, and deliver enhanced capabilities to query and analyze the BSA data. This vision directly supports the Section 361 mandate and FinCEN's mission by promoting increased and efficient use of BSA data.

The Internal Revenue Service (IRS), through its Detroit Computing Center (DCC), has served as Treasury's central repository for all BSA related data. The DCC maintains the Information Technology (IT) infrastructure and operations support needed to collect the BSA reports, convert paper and magnetic tape submissions to electronic media, and correct errors in submitted forms through correspondence with filers. The DCC also maintains BSA data storage and retrieval systems and provides BSA information verification and certification.

Today, one of FinCEN's primary methods for providing customers with access to BSA data is the Gateway program, which allows users to access the IRS data retrieval system, the Currency and Banking Retrieval System (CBRS), using a secure web application called Secure Outreach. Until recently, however, access to the IRS-hosted BSA database system has been cumbersome with limited options for querying the data. In late 2005, the IRS significantly improved the situation by beginning the deployment of a new web-based version of CBRS called WebCBRS.

FinCEN developed the concept of BSA Direct R&S in 2003 as an alternative to the legacy version of CBRS, with the goal of improving the BSA data retrieval processes. The project was to build a secure data warehouse to consolidate BSA data into a single, integrated data set, and develop a flexible and robust query system accessible through an intuitive web interface. FinCEN intended to provide additional and more flexible capabilities than those now available (including through WebCBRS), by allowing end users to perform both ad hoc and pre-defined queries and reporting. FinCEN envisioned BSA Direct R&S as a best-of-breed data management and retrieval system to accomplish the following objectives:

---

[2] 31 U.S.C. §310(b)(2)(B)(i).

- Address the needs of FinCEN customers for easier data access by providing single sign-on access via an easy-to-use web interface;
- Integrate COTS business intelligence tools so that customers could analyze data online;
- Establish the capability for consolidating direct access to the BSA data for FinCEN's analysts and external customers;
- Address requirements for a high level of data quality using data cleansing and transformation technology; and
- Include processes, capability enhancements, and technologies aligned with FinCEN's enterprise modernization requirements.

Last, but not least, BSA Direct R&S represented a strategic initiative in the truest sense, intended to eventually interface with BSA e-Filing and other functionality necessary to transition all BSA reporting and data related processes from the IRS to FinCEN over time. FinCEN expected BSA Direct R&S to increase its ability to network agencies with overlapping interests and to augment its ability to audit and assess the usage of BSA data.

In early 2003, FinCEN issued a Request for Information (RFI) to industry for the development, hosting, secure access, and management of all BSA databases in a secure web-based environment.[3] Based on the responses to the RFI, FinCEN issued a Request for Proposals (RFP) in November 2003 for the analysis, design, and deployment of BSA Direct R&S, as well as for web hosting services and the operations and maintenance of the system. As stated in the RFP, FinCEN anticipated that the successful offeror would rely heavily on COTS software. The solicitation process culminated with an award to the Contractor on June 30, 2004, to develop the initial operating capability (IOC) for $8.9 million, with option years for O&M.

The BSA Direct R&S project has experienced cost overruns and ongoing schedule delays as well as issues concerning de-scoping of contract requirements in an effort to meet an aggressive schedule. As a result of these issues and other concerns, such as invalidated data quality, poor system performance, erratic system testing, and inadequate security documentation, FinCEN's Director decided on March 15, 2006, that a temporary stop-work order should be issued in order to perform an assessment of the BSA Direct R&S project.

Two teams conducted assessments over a period of 120 days. i2S, Inc. executed an independent technical assessment, and FinCEN, with the assistance of SiloSmashers, Inc., conducted a comprehensive assessment, whose findings and recommendations are presented in this paper and in the accompanying BSA Direct R&S Technical System Assessment. Both teams, working separately, analyzed an accumulation of project documentation, interviewed BSA Direct R&S project management and staff, and observed the BSA Direct R&S system in its current state.

The results of the assessments indicate that the underlying vision of BSA Direct R&S is still valid, namely that FinCEN should use currently available technology to improve the quality, management and use of BSA data. However, in its present state BSA Direct R&S does not fulfill this vision and is not ready for deployment to FinCEN's internal or external users for reasons detailed in the body of this report.

---

[3] FinCEN received responses from a number of well-known companies, including SAIC, Northrop Grumman, and EDS, all of whom suggested a data warehouse solution of one form or another.

3.0   Findings

3.1   Overview

BSA Direct R&S was a high-risk project from the start, given its broad scope and ostensibly immovable deadline. Although FinCEN staff and management worked diligently to deliver this important project, problems ensued from which the project could not recover. Neither FinCEN nor the Contractor clearly understood the scope of work at a sufficiently detailed level to project an accurate end date with any degree of confidence. The project management principle of the "triple constraint" provides that scope, schedule, and resources are project factors that are directly related to and influence each other; therefore, if one of these constraints changes, then at least one of the other two constraints must also change. The findings show that both FinCEN and the Contractor ignored this basic, critical project management principle.

From the project's inception, FinCEN management emphasized the criticality of meeting the scheduled delivery date of October 14, 2005. As FinCEN and the Contractor came to understand the scope of the project and as the requirements expanded, executives from both parties continued to reinforce the need to meet the desired end date. Other problems arose that further affected the schedule, including staffing delays by the Government and Contractor, missing requirements, system performance inadequacies, and COTS integration issues. However, both parties were committed to the original end date. Over time, work was repeatedly deferred to later in the project, and the schedule became more compressed. As a result, there was not enough time to thoroughly review important project artifacts and confirm critical design decisions. Pressure on FinCEN and Contractor staff intensified, risk increased, milestones slipped, costs increased, and quality degraded.   The result is that BSA Direct R&S is a partially built system, which inadequately integrates a number of best-in-class products, which do not function well together. It represents a system that, as currently configured, cannot be provided to any of FinCEN's users.

The findings below summarize the results of the BSA Direct R&S assessment and support the conclusions described above.

3.2   Overly Aggressive Schedule

▫ **End date set before completion of procurement**: Interviews with FinCEN representatives indicate that the original Government estimate for the project duration was eighteen months to two years. A FinCEN risk matrix for the project, dated March 11, 2004, states that "the project could readily be completed by 9/30/05, if begun by 4/1/04. In order to begin by 4/1/04, contract must be awarded by 3/15/04, which means that the RFP should have been issued by 12/1/03." When the solicitation for BSA Direct R&S was issued in February 2004, over two months later than planned, it still specified a required end date of September 30, 2005.   The contract was not awarded until June 30, 2004 over three months later than projected, but in accordance with executive direction, the expected delivery date was not extended for a commensurate length of time. The Contractor agreed to deliver the project by

October 14, 2005 – in fifteen months. As the project progressed, despite the fact that both FinCEN and the Contractor were aware of the need for adjustment, the original contract end date was not revised accordingly.

▫ **Key milestone dates missed, while end date remained the same**: The IV&V consultants from MITRE developed a matrix that summarizes the BSA Direct R&S schedule changes by month. The Contractor planned to deliver BSA Direct R&S in three iterations, with Iteration 3 providing the Initial Operating Capability (IOC) on October 14, 2005. The matrix reflects that, from September 2004 through July 2005, projected completion dates for Iteration 1 and Iteration 2 were extended by two months, while the Iteration 3 IOC date remained at October 14, 2005.

▫ **New baseline established, but pattern of missing milestones continued**: In September 2005, the Contractor and FinCEN agreed to re-baseline the project plan. The new plan extended the delivery date to April 28, 2006. However, from September 2005 to February 2006 the pattern of slippage continued; the dates of interim milestones continued to slip while the April 28, 2006 delivery date did not change.

▫ **Scope devolved as requirements were deviated from or not fully developed**: As time progressed, functionality and defect resolution were pushed to the end of the schedule. It was not until February 2006, two months before the planned delivery date, that the Contractor proposed major scope reductions to meet the April 28, 2006 deadline. The February schedule proposed combining the last two iterations and deferring key requirements, such as download capabilities, scheduling of queries, network redundancy, a separate training system, and automated data transfer capabilities. FinCEN identified major issues and risks with the proposed iteration compression and scope reduction, and determined that it would be unrealistic to continue the project based on user acceptance risks and schedule instability.

3.3   Significant Increase in Overall Project Cost

▫ **Cost increases incurred:** The original budget for the project was $8,982,985 and increased to $15,146,289 before the stop-work order was issued. The latest estimate, however, was based on an April 28, 2006 delivery date, which was considered highly unlikely due to the large number of unresolved defects and unsatisfied requirements. The majority of the cost increases, $4,210,586, was due to software and hardware cost escalations and a contract schedule extension to complete the project. The addition of the Gateway functionality, a component that was not clearly articulated in the Statement of Work (SOW) and was not included in the Contractor's cost proposal, increased the budget by $925,523 (described in Section 3.4).

▫ **Costs for delivery likely to rise:** The level of effort and costs necessary to complete the project requirements and address all remaining defects are most likely greater than the latest projections show. The Contractor's February 2006 monthly status report included an estimate at completion (EAC) of $15.1 million. This figure, however, is highly improbable since the actual project costs through the date of the stop-work order were $14.4 million. In January 2006, MITRE executed an analysis of the "BSA Direct Schedule Most Likely Trend" that projected the total final costs at $22,939,144, including $3,000,000 for hardware and software upgrades, as well as the Contractor's average monthly costs of $650,000.

▫ **Costs for O&M likely to rise:** The projections for O&M were initially budgeted at between $1.8 and $2.1 million. In a March 2006 meeting, the contractor Project Manager (PM) advised the FinCEN PM and Contracting Officer's Technical Representative (COTR) that the original projections would be insufficient to support the project going forward and would need to be reassessed. As a result, there is currently no accurate projection of future O&M costs.

3.4   Unclear Project Scope and Requirements

▫ **Functional and user requirements based on FinCEN preliminary requirements document:** During the BSA Direct R&S procurement, FinCEN established a user requirements working group to develop a document called "Preliminary User Requirements Analysis for BSA Direct." The purpose of the document was to accelerate the requirements analysis phase of the contractor's work. FinCEN expected the Contractor to conduct in-depth user sessions to augment the FinCEN preliminary requirements and meet the level of requirements detail specified in the SOW. The Contractor, however, based the Iteration 1 functional and system requirements on the preliminary requirements, and conducted very few requirements sessions. Although the FinCEN preliminary requirements provided a thorough view of the "as-is" environment, with sections on desired features from BSA Direct R&S, they did not describe the detailed requirements needed to accurately scope and plan the work for BSA Direct R&S.

▫ **Iteration 1 requirements focused only on ad hoc query requirements:** Iteration 1 requirements focused on the ad hoc query functionality that was described in the SOW. Although the FinCEN COTR signed off on the Iteration 1 requirements in January 2005, the project team and users verified in April 2005, that the ad hoc functionality did not satisfy the majority of the users who simply need an easy query. The Contractor agreed to include custom screens to accommodate this simple query functionality, referred to as "EZ Query." The result was structured, simple query functionality, retrofitted into a platform designed for advanced analytics. Although this effort increased the complexity of the project, the schedule end date was not revised to accommodate the additional work required to incorporate this feature into BSA Direct R&S.

▫ **Requirements for Gateway component were added to the project for Iteration 2:** The Gateway component is a major function that is not clearly defined in the SOW and was not included in the Contractor's cost proposal. This module tracks case data and supports the networking of users researching the same case. In March of 2005, the contract was modified to add this functionality with associated funding. The Contractor added a new team to develop the Gateway component. Although this component added project requirements and complexity, the schedule end date was not changed at this time.

▫ **Key requirement for executing queries against structured and unstructured data not easily supported by the system:** A key requirement of FinCEN BSA data users that is not supported by the current system, but is supported by WebCBRS, is the ability to search unstructured (narrative) text data along with structured (fixed fields) data in a single query. The SOW requires that the system "provide the ability to search for the text in lengthy narrative fields, with Boolean operators and wildcards, separately or in conjunction with searches on other data fields, quickly, and with the search returns highlighted in the response." The BSA Direct R&S architecture included two COTS packages for queries, one for structured data and one for unstructured text data. However, the solution did not allow both kinds of searches within one query. When FinCEN project staff discovered that this functionality was missing, they stressed its criticality to the Contractor. The Contractor evaluated alternatives, but all suitable options increased costs and required several months of development. Although the lack of this functionality represented a risk to user acceptance, the requirement was deferred to a future iteration based upon the perceived impact to the project schedule and budget.

3.5 Inadequate Project Governance

▫ **FinCEN executives were involved, but did not address emerging risks and issues**: The FinCEN PM reported that at the beginning of the project there were no regular status meetings with senior management. There was no sanctioned Steering Committee with defined roles and responsibilities in relation to the project. As the project progressed, the FinCEN PM conducted weekly meetings with FinCEN executives, including the Director, Deputy Director, numerous Assistant Directors, the Contracting Officer, the Budget Officer, the Chief Information Officer (CIO), the Deputy CIO, and the Chief of Staff, to report project status, risks, and issues. However, FinCEN project staff report that executives were not receptive to hearing about risks and issues. The executives' main emphasis was on making the schedule deadlines, instead of working to resolve issues and mitigate risks.

▫ **IV&V contractor raised schedule risks, but end date was not changed**: In April 2005, the IV&V contractor, MITRE, conducted an independent schedule analysis using Monte Carlo simulations and presented the results to FinCEN management. The first comprehensive IV&V analysis, dated April 2005 showed low confidence in the Contractor's ability to meet the October 14, 2005 delivery date. At that time, MITRE projected the most likely deployment date to be January 2006. To make the October 14, 2005 delivery date, the Contractor proposed combining Iterations 2 and 3. FinCEN's then-senior executives chose to reject the MITRE findings and the Contractor's proposal to reduce project scope. Instead, they took the high-risk approach of maintaining the original delivery date, without reduction in scope. The Contractor articulated that it would continue to work toward the October 14, 2005 date, as directed, but would need to bring on additional resources to meet the schedule.

▫ **Lack of Stakeholder Inclusion and Agreement**: Although the project had FinCEN executive commitment, it did not have the buy-in of the majority of the FinCEN stakeholders. For example, although the SOW required a complex analytical capability, the majority of stakeholders, once they saw the system, stated that the primary capability they required was an easy-to-use, structured query. In addition, although FinCEN designated a project sponsor - typically a key role to ensure organizational buy-in and compliance with business needs - the sponsor was not actively involved. Further, the project did not have a designated user group with a leader assigned throughout the project to address user needs. In addition, the majority of FinCEN IT staff required to support the project were not involved in the SOW or the initial project activities. As BSA Direct R&S progressed, FinCEN IT staff became more involved and began to identify missing requirements. From this, the Assessment Team concludes that, had the IT staff been involved earlier, FinCEN would have clearly avoided some costly requirements omissions.

3.6   Lack of Demonstrated Project Management Expertise by Both the Contractor and FinCEN

▫ **Contractor did not accurately estimate schedule**: The Contractor experienced challenges with schedule management. Over the course of twenty-plus months, the project had three different Contractor PMs, none of whom was able to effectively control the scope and meet schedule milestones. Although the SOW required a baseline plan and master schedule within 40 days of contract award, the Contractor did not deliver a baseline schedule that was accepted by FinCEN until December 2004, six months after the project was initiated and after 40% of the proposed project duration was expended. Project milestones continuously slipped thereafter. As described in Section 3.2, in September 2005, FinCEN agreed to extend the end date to April 28, 2006, but that end date still did not accurately reflect the scope of work to be completed, as revealed through subsequent schedule slippages. It was not until February 2006 that the Contractor PM attempted to compensate for the compressed schedule, while continuing to meet the April 28, 2006 delivery date, by proposing a substantial scope decrease.

▫ **Contractor performance lacked evidence of CMMI® Level 2 processes, as required in the SOW and the contractor proposal:** The BSA Direct R&S SOW requires that the contractor team assigned to the project be Software Engineering Institute (SEI) Capability Maturity Model® Integration (CMMI) Level 2 certified. The Contractor's proposal committed to this requirement, and its project management planning documents included processes and procedures commensurate with CMMI Level 2[4]. The project, however, lacked evidence of effective execution of the processes defined in the plans. According to the SEI text, "CMMI Guidelines for Process Integration and Product Improvement," CMMI Level 2 processes ensure, "that requirements are managed and that processes are planned, performed, measured, and controlled….that existing practices are retained during times of stress. When these practices are in place, projects are performed and managed according to their documented plans."

---

[4] This finding does not reflect a formal SEI evaluation. It is based on opinions of FinCEN project management and staff involved in the project.

- **Project lacked effective scope management:** As described in Section 3.4, FinCEN did not clearly define the scope of BSA Direct R&S in the SOW, which resulted in added requirements as the project progressed. FinCEN did not establish change management processes, typically utilized to manage and control scope. In addition, FinCEN did not establish a Change Control Board (CCB), through which management would review and approve or disapprove changes to the schedule, scope, and budget. Nor did the Bureau establish change control processes to document and analyze ongoing requirement changes and their impacts to the project. Although the Contractor held internal change control meetings, they did not invite FinCEN staff to participate. Furthermore, the Contractor did not effectively convey to FinCEN the full impact that added requirements had on the schedule.

- **Earned Value Management controls were not effective:** In its December 2004 and January 2005 IV&V reports, MITRE stated that the Contractor's earned value process and fundamentals were flawed. FinCEN project staff noted that MITRE personnel assisted in educating the Government and contractor staff in earned value. The Contractor did not issue the first earned value report until January 2005, seven months into the project. The earned value report variances fluctuated from month to month, and did not reflect effectively the true health of the project, nor did they correlate with the schedule slippages and scope deferrals described in other management reports.

3.7 Issues and Delays in Fully Staffing the Project by the Contractor and FinCEN

- **Contractor staffing delayed due to security clearance:** From the outset, the Contractor had difficulty identifying staff with the required security clearance. Until September 2005, MITRE stated in its monthly IV&V reports that "inadequate staffing continues to impact project progress." Eventually FinCEN lessened the security requirements, but this could not compensate for over one year of related staffing issues.

- **FinCEN understaffed the project:** BSA Direct R&S was an aggressive project with scope, schedule, and cost challenges from the start, and as a result required full-time FinCEN support. In the first months of the project, both the FinCEN PM and COTR served in multiple capacities. The PM also functioned as an IT Management Official and the COTR as the Chief Technologist for the Bureau. In February 2005 FinCEN assigned a different PM, but the replacement also served in multiple roles. It was not until September 2005, when FinCEN relieved the PM of her other duties, that BSA Direct R&S had a full-time Government PM. In addition, the project lacked dedicated IT staff until November 2005, when FinCEN assigned two full-time technologists. Furthermore, there was no designated end user champion, nor were there end users who were consistently assigned to the project.

- **Contractor staff turnover impacted project:** The Contractor encountered problems with staff turnover. The Contractor assigned three PMs over the course of the project, in addition to experiencing turnover with requirements analysts, test managers, configuration managers and data modelers. Also, some of the key technical leads for the Contractor were reassigned to other projects within the company, and replaced with personnel having lower skill levels.

3.8   Underestimation of the Time and Complexity Required for COTS Integration

▫ **Project based on complex integration of many COTS packages**: The BSA Direct R&S system architecture is based on a complex integration of many high-level COTS packages. As noted in the BSA Direct R&S Technical System Assessment, the solution required much more customization and design work-arounds to meet FinCEN requirements than was originally estimated by the contractor. Individually, these products provide very robust functional capabilities and scalability to support long-term, complex, data analysis requirements. However, the complexity of integrating the products during the BSA Direct R&S project resulted in design tradeoffs, schedule increases, and decreased system quality.

▫ **Problems encountered with Business Objects™ analysis package**: One of the primary sources of integration problems was Business Objects™, a leading business intelligence product widely used across federal civilian agencies. Business Objects™ provides robust capabilities for complex queries of structured data, but adds additional complexity and performance overhead for simple queries, which represent the bulk of BSA Direct R&S user needs. To address some of the problems, the Contractor recommended a new version of Business Objects™ that included enhanced integration capabilities. FinCEN agreed to the Contractor's recommendation. Unfortunately, however, the Contractor did not have staff experienced with the new version and the software did not seem mature. Resolving issues with Business Objects™ required more time than the Contractor originally scheduled, and the result did not meet FinCEN needs for user-friendliness and performance.

3.9   Unacceptable System Quality

▫ **Iteration 1 completed without resolving major system issues:** There were differences of opinion between FinCEN and the Contractor, as noted in the BSA Direct R&S Technical System Assessment, about the approach to Iteration 1 testing.   While FinCEN project staff believed that each iteration would not be complete until all requirements for that iteration were fully developed, tested and major problems corrected, the Contractor's approach was to refine the implementation of requirements and correct problems in later increments, with no clear acceptance criteria/quality gates for the iteration. The FinCEN team reports that, for Iteration 1, only 59 of 122 planned test scripts were executed (48%), and only 30 of those 59 passed (51%). The Contractor's decision to begin Iteration 2 before correcting the Iteration 1 defects pushed effort and risk into a future release, further compressing the schedule. The result was that the Contractor built Iteration 2 on an unstable Iteration 1 foundation.

▫ **Data Architecture activities impacted by the aggressive schedule**: As noted in the BSA Direct R&S Technical System Assessment, there was a disagreement between the Contractor and FinCEN about the approach to the logical and physical data models that form the foundation of the data warehouse. This disagreement was not resolved quickly and delayed the project. The Contractor contended that it proposed an iterative approach to the model, while FinCEN decided that a fully integrated model was required for Iteration 1. The Contractor asserted that FinCEN's data model activities increased the schedule by eight weeks and had a rippling effect on Iteration 1 activities. FinCEN project staff, however, stated that the Contractor did not deliver an acceptable data model, so FinCEN provided an alternative model. Ultimately, the Contractor used the data model recommended by FinCEN. Since FinCEN has not defined long-term data requirements, the viability of the model to support future business needs is uncertain. In its present form, the data warehouse does not consolidate or accommodate the current FinCEN BSA data repository[5], but represents a second replicated BSA database at FinCEN.

- **Iteration 2 User Acceptance Testing (UAT) began before system issues were resolved:** FinCEN staff had just begun UAT for Iteration 2 when the stop-work order was issued. According to FinCEN staff, the Bureau cancelled UAT on the first day because of outdated test scripts and issues with user IDs for role-level access. FinCEN staff reported that the Contractor started UAT with many severity 1 defects unresolved. Also, both the FinCEN Test Lead and MITRE documented concerns with the depth and quality of the Contractor test scripts. The Contractor never performed a full regression test, nor did it execute a full performance load test. Because of incomplete testing throughout the project life cycle, the amount of time and resources necessary to fix remaining significant issues is unknown.

- **Performance requirements not met by the system:** System performance is one of the biggest problems cited by FinCEN users. They expressed concerns throughout Iteration 1 testing that simple queries took too long to execute. As noted in the BSA Direct R&S Technical System Assessment, in some cases response times for simple queries through BSA Direct R&S were several times slower than the IRS legacy CBRS or new WebCBRS system. Although the Contractor greatly improved response time over the course of the project, it was still unacceptable at the time of the stop-work order. It is unclear whether the Contractor can tune the system to a level of performance that will meet user expectations and, if so, what it would entail in terms of funding and additional expenditure of time.

- **Data quality uncertain:** Although the Assessment Team could not assess the quality of the data because testing had not progressed far enough to conduct a full evaluation, several incidents bring the quality of the data into question. First, during Iteration 1 testing, which was to include ten-plus years of historical data, the Contractor provided FinCEN testers an extract of only 1,200 records for testing. Because this sample represented less than .01% of the data, Government staff felt it was inadequate to identify potential data anomalies. Second, in January 2006, FinCEN staff identified data anomalies, captured in error files, that were never reviewed by the Contractor. At the time of the stop-work, the Contractor had defined business rules to address these problems, but had not reloaded the ten years of data with the new business rules to test their effectiveness. Third, in March 2006, FinCEN

---

[5] Today, FinCEN maintains a copy of the BSA Data, used with the VisuaLinks® software package, for internal users to conduct complex analytics and data linkage studies.

identified problems with the capture and storage of date of death, a key search criterion that the Contractor had not addressed.

4.0   Options

Based on its findings, the Assessment Team evaluated three options for the future of BSA Direct R&S. All three of the options continue the vision for BSA Direct R&S. Although the execution of the BSA Direct R&S project was flawed, the vision for BSA Direct R&S nonetheless remains valid. FinCEN must continue to pursue greater control of the budget and processes surrounding BSA data collection and processing, improve BSA data quality, and provide enhanced capabilities to query and analyze the BSA data for both internal and external customers.

The three options devised by the Assessment Team are described below. The team estimated costs for each of the options. The costs are an estimate, based on the currently understood status of the system. Furthermore, all costs below are in addition to the $14.4 million already expended on BSA Direct R&S.

Option 1 - Continue BSA Direct R&S with the current contractor: This option resumes work with the Contractor based on renegotiated terms and conditions of the contract to include a new project schedule and revision to the cost plus fixed fee arrangement that was originally established for the contract.

The Assessment Team estimates that it would take the Contractor at least four months to re-launch the BSA Direct R&S project based on a need to allocate new staff to replace team members that have now been assigned to other projects. The projected development and deployment time takes into account the resolution of the known severe system defects, additional unknown defects that will most likely be discovered as further tests are performed, and the integration of critical functionalities deferred at the end of the project (structured/unstructured queries, scheduled queries, download capability, etc.).

Assuming four months for ramp-up, eight months for development/deployment time, and an August 1, 2006 start date, BSA Direct R&S would be delivered in August 2007.

- **Cost Estimates**:
  - The estimate to complete the project, while meeting the current set of identified requirements, is an additional $8 million. This estimate is based on the current Contractor rates and includes IV&V costs, as well as hardware and software fees[6].
  - The estimate for ongoing O&M costs is at least $2.5 million, based on the Contractor's statements that the original estimates of $1.8 to $2.1 million per year were underestimated.

- **Benefits**:
  - Takes advantage of sunken hardware and software costs.
  - Less vendor knowledge transfer required than if FinCEN continues with new contractor.

---

[6] This estimate is different than the one provided by MITRE, referenced in Section 3.3 of the Findings, in that this estimate takes into account the stop-work order and the resulting staff ramp-up that would be required by the Contractor. MITRE's estimate in January 2006 was based on a continuation of the established Contractor team. In addition, this estimate does not include the Teradata software upgrade that MITRE added to its estimates, because the Assessment Team did not find documentation to substantiate that the upgrade is required.

□ **Risks**:
- High risk with current Contractor and history that delivery will not be acceptable.
- High risk that current architecture/solution will not meet requirements.
- FinCEN does not yet have the staff with the technical or project management expertise to support this effort.

Option 2 - Continue BSA Direct R&S with a new contractor: This option terminates the agreement with the existing contractor. It also requires a new procurement action providing the partially built BSA Direct R&S system as Government furnished equipment to the new contractor. This option would provide an opportunity to leverage the hard-won knowledge about the BSA Direct R&S project and remedy contractual shortcomings with a new performance-based vehicle. The new contractor would be required to validate requirements and revisit the original design and technology solution, salvaging components wherever possible. This option includes a new procurement, estimated to take approximately six months.

Assuming six months for the procurement, four months for ramp-up, eleven months for requirements/design validation and development/deployment time, and a start date of August 1, 2006 would result in delivery of BSA Direct R&S in May 2008.

□ **Cost Estimates**:
- The estimate to complete the project, while meeting the current set of identified requirements, is an additional $10 million. This estimate includes contractor support for the procurement, assumes the same rates as the current contractor, includes time to validate the requirements and design, costs for relocation of the existing equipment, IV&V costs, and hardware and software fees.
- As no other data is available, the estimate for ongoing O&M costs is at least $2.5 million, the same as Option 1.

□ **Benefits**:
- Takes advantage of sunken hardware and software costs.
- Provides a fresh perspective from a new vendor.

□ **Risks**:
- Requires additional time for vendor knowledge transfer and validation of requirements and design.
- High risk that current architecture/solution will not meet requirements.
- FinCEN does not yet have the staff with the technical or project management expertise to support this effort.

Option 3 – Reassess the project and plan for new capabilities: This option terminates the existing agreement with the Contractor, but unlike Option 2, provides for a planning effort to re-scope the entire BSA Direct R&S effort. It includes a reassessment of business and user needs, a reprioritization of objectives, and the development of a plan to execute BSA Direct R&S through a phased approach comprised of a series of discrete projects.

As this option includes re-planning, and potentially a different system solution and approach, the estimates below are confined to a limited scope of work that can be reasonably assumed. The limited scope includes a stakeholder analysis, re-planning, and the development of the FinCEN data warehouse. The warehouse would subsume the legacy FinCEN repository currently supporting complex internal analytics and would leverage the data processing and analytical tools from the current project. Assuming six months for procurement activities, six months for stakeholder analysis and re-planning, twelve months for the design and delivery of the data warehouse, and a start date of August 1, 2006, the BSA Direct R&S warehouse would be delivered in August 2008.

▫ **Costs**: The estimate to conduct the analysis and planning activities and to deliver a FinCEN BSA Direct R&S data warehouse is approximately $7 million. This estimate includes contractor support for procurement activities, stakeholder analysis, re-planning, and the design and development of the data warehouse. It also includes costs for relocation/hosting of the existing equipment, IV&V costs, and hardware and software fees.

▫ **Benefits**:
- Saves additional costs expended on a potentially wrong solution.
- Salvages reusable components of the existing system.
- Advances BSA Direct R&S Concept.
- Incorporates current legacy repository, consolidating maintenance costs.
- Gives FinCEN time to improve its project management discipline, advance its Enterprise Architecture, and organize a staffing structure to support this effort.

▫ **Risks**:
- Delivery of end-to-end solution takes longer than other options.

5.0 Recommendations

5.1 Overview

The recommendation of the Assessment Team is **Option 3 – Reassess the project and plan for new capabilities.** The Assessment Team's findings support the position that BSA Direct R&S, as currently envisioned and configured, does not satisfy present and future FinCEN user requirements. Furthermore, those user requirements will be costly and cumbersome to retrofit into the current architecture. Option 3 includes the evaluation of stakeholder needs, the incorporation of lessons learned, and the development of a plan to satisfy BSA Direct R&S objectives over time, as a series of initiatives that are directly tied to FinCEN strategic goals and objectives. Because the IRS DCC maintains the data collection and processing of the BSA data and the WebCBRS data access system, it will be critical for FinCEN to cooperate closely with IRS DCC in pursuing the realization of the BSA Direct R&S vision through this option.

The components of Option 3 and their associated benefits are described below.

□ **Reassessment of business and user needs:** Option 3 includes a reassessment of business and user needs, and a reprioritization of objectives. A major hindrance to BSA Direct R&S was the lack of stakeholder support. The goal of the system was to increase the use of BSA data by providing advanced analytical capabilities to end users. The SOW described this functionality and the contractor proposed a solution to satisfy this request. However, after reviewing the system, the project team and the user test group concluded that it did not meet the needs of the majority of users who require only simple, structured queries with fast performance. An analysis of the present and future requirements of external users, fully communicated to all stakeholders, will define the needed BSA Direct R&S capabilities and strengthen user support.

The business environment has changed since the inception of BSA Direct R&S. During the reassessment of business and user needs, the following factors must be taken into consideration to ensure they are included in the re-planning of BSA Direct R&S:

- The IRS has implemented WebCBRS, a promising application for basic query and download of BSA data.

- Some agencies require their own copies of the BSA data so they can integrate it with other data sources to maximize value. For example, the FBI maintains a copy of the BSA data in its Investigative Data Warehouse (IDW) and integrates it with over 50 different data set sources. The value of BSA data is disproportionate to its volume. For instance, although the BSA data comprises only 15% of the documents, it represents 40% of the queries and usage is increasing.

Option 3 includes analysis and re-planning to understand current and future needs of all users, and to develop approaches that meet those needs. It will take into consideration the WebCBRS system, the needs and controls for downloaded data stores, internal FinCEN users, and the varying needs of the external user community.

- **Development of the solution in modular phases:** One of the Assessment Team's major findings is that BSA Direct R&S was conceived with an overly aggressive schedule; it was one project with many components whose true scope and requirements were not well understood. As a result, the project suffered compromises to critical foundation components like the data warehouse structure and data quality as the pressure for FinCEN and the contractor to meet the schedule loomed. Option 3 recommends that the BSA Direct R&S vision be accomplished in steps, as a program, with multiple projects – both business-oriented and technology-oriented – to achieve the desired state. One of the advantages of this approach is the potential to reuse the salvageable components of the existing system through small projects in a relatively short timeframe.

- **Improvement of FinCEN capabilities to support BSA Direct R&S:** The BSA Direct R&S assessment findings provide lessons learned for FinCEN as it moves to fulfill the BSA Direct R&S vision. FinCEN is a young organization with immature project management and information technology disciplines. Option 3 includes a modular approach over time that will allow FinCEN to improve its capabilities in these areas to better support the future BSA Direct R&S program. FinCEN is in the process of hiring a Chief Information Officer, building a data quality program, developing a Program Management Office, expanding its Enterprise Architecture, and improving its Capital Planning and Investment Control function.

- **Understanding of internal user needs from the start:** The re-planning will take into consideration FinCEN's internal needs for complex analytics. Today, FinCEN maintains a copy of BSA data, used with the VisuaLinks® analytical tool for complex analysis and data linkage. Its use has grown and improved since BSA Direct R&S was envisioned. VisuaLinks® is a vital tool for some analysts, and FinCEN must do more to ensure confidence in the data used with VisuaLinks®.

5.2 Current Actions

Currently, FinCEN is actively working to ensure business continuity, formalize its relationship with the IRS, implement a data quality program, and mature its Enterprise Architecture (EA) and project management discipline.

- **Ensure business continuity by converting from CBRS to WebCBRS:** FinCEN has kicked off this project and is on track to convert all users to WebCBRS by September 2006. The application has been well received by those who have used it. It actually represents a first step in achievement of the BSA Direct R&S vision, because WebCBRS provides end users easier access and improved functionality for BSA data than the current CBRS system.

- **Continue relationship with IRS DCC:** This relationship is especially important now that FinCEN will convert its users to WebCBRS. FinCEN did not actively engage in discussions with the IRS about WebCBRS as it was being developed, so FinCEN-specific requirements were not included. To remedy this, FinCEN must be an active participant in specifying and prioritizing the ongoing enhancements to WebCBRS. Discussions currently occur with the IRS about issues with data extracts (to populate the VisuaLinks® database) and e-filing transmissions (electronic BSA data transmission function owned and managed by FinCEN).

In addition, in recent meetings, the IRS indicated that it is possible to add additional data fields or derived data to the database.

FinCEN must mitigate the risk that historical issues between FinCEN and the IRS will resurface, as FinCEN becomes a major user of WebCBRS. Although FinCEN is responsible for the management, collection, processing, and dissemination of BSA data, the IRS currently performs many of these functions as a service provider to FinCEN. The relationship between FinCEN and the IRS has been problematic in the past, because the governance of this association has not been updated to keep pace with new requirements, processes and procedures. As recommended in Section 5.4, FinCEN and the IRS should formalize governance by establishing a charter that clearly delineates roles and responsibilities. In addition, FinCEN should consider coordinating its interactions with the IRS under a designated FinCEN lead, whose responsibilities would be defined in the charter.

- **Establish a Program Management Office (PMO):** FinCEN is currently in the solicitation phase for contractor support to develop processes and implement a PMO. The PMO will provide a structure to standardize project management practices, facilitate IT project portfolio management, provide project planning tools and methods, and perform review and analysis of projects. The PMO can incorporate a view of all projects and help manage cross project resources and dependencies. Additionally, since FinCEN has engaged external service providers to outsource most of its application development and O&M work, the PMO should include processes for vendor acquisition and management.

- **Improve BSA Data Quality:** FinCEN is significantly increasing its efforts at improving BSA data quality, starting with a review of the internal processes employed at FinCEN to transform and load data into the BSA data repository it maintains for complex data analysis.

- **Develop Enterprise Architecture:** FinCEN is continuing its EA development, as required by the Treasury Department and Office of Management and Budget. FinCEN began this effort by completing the "As-Is" phase of the EA in 2003 and is hiring an experienced enterprise architect to lead the development of the "To-Be" architecture. To ensure FinCEN's alignment with the Department of the Treasury EA, FinCEN is continuing to participate in the Treasury Department's Treasury EA Committee, which is sponsored by Treasury's CIO Council. Furthermore, in 2006 FinCEN intends to leverage the new Treasury blanket purchase agreement to provide support services for the use of the Metis® EA tool.

5.3   Short-Term Recommendations

Short-term recommendations are those that can be accomplished within the next nine months.

▫ **End contract with the contractor:** The first step is to end formally the contract with the contractor. The activities include the necessary contractual steps to discontinue the contractor's services.

▫ **Evaluate the components of the BSA Direct R&S project for salvageability:** FinCEN will need to make an inventory of all of the hardware, software, and delivered artifacts for BSA Direct R&S.

- **Hardware:** The costs and licenses will need to be understood and tracked. FinCEN will need to determine which servers, routers, etc. can be reused on other projects.

- **Software:** The cost and license agreements will need to be tracked. Although several of the software packages may be useful, FinCEN will need to evaluate whether the software can and will be used and in what timeframe. A cost/benefit analysis should be performed to determine whether maintaining the software is justified.

  Software includes:

  o **Ascential® -** Data Extract, Transform and Load (ETL) tool.

  o **Autonomy® -** Used to perform advanced searches against the narrative text data.

  o **Acxiom® -** Supplies business reference data on a monthly basis.

  o **Business Objects™ XI -** Business intelligence (BI) platform that delivers a complete set of BI capabilities: reporting, query and analysis, performance management, and data integration.

  o **Computer Associates (CA™) eTrust® Antivirus Version 6.0 -**Antivirus application used to detect and remove computer viruses.

  o **F5 Networks™ BIG-IP® 520 Server Appliances –** Internet Traffic and Content Management product that provides comprehensive traffic management and load balancing to intelligently direct Internet Protocol traffic to the most optimal resource (server/application).

  o **Intrusion Detection System (IDS) –** An IDS inspects all inbound and outbound network activity and identifies suspicious patterns that may indicate a network or system attack from someone attempting to break into or compromise a system. Cisco Systems provided this component.

  o **Teradata® -** Provides integrated, optimized and extensible enterprise data warehouse technology and services.

  o **Vignette® –** Portal functionality.

- **Artifacts:** This includes all of the documentation delivered by the contractor, such as requirements documents, design documents, data models, data business rules, training plans, etc. FinCEN will need to catalogue and store these artifacts. The documentation will most likely be salvageable as a starting point for future artifacts. The data-oriented artifacts will probably be the most effective in the short term, to support FinCEN's data quality program. In addition, the lessons learned about the data business rules are valuable and useful. FinCEN staff has acknowledged that the Help Desk procedures and online training processes are already being reused.

- **Code:** This includes the modules that were developed to create the Gateway component, and code written to support the COTS packages. The most likely candidate for reuse is the Ascential® code, written to extract, transform, and load the data from DCC to FinCEN. The ETL functionality most likely will be required in the future to support FinCEN's data repository.

▫ **Conduct Re-planning:** FinCEN should formalize a re-planning project for BSA Direct R&S. The project should include a charter, a designated PM, and dedicated resources. The goal is to review the strategic objectives for BSA Direct R&S and to develop a roadmap to achieve the BSA Direct R&S vision. The recommended re-planning activities include:

- **Strategy Planning** – Revisit the strategic plan to redefine the strategic goals for BSA data collection, processing, analysis and dissemination.

- **Solution Review** – Develop the business strategy to determine what technology, automation, streamlined business processes, and investments need to be accomplished in order to meet the strategic goals for BSA Direct R&S. This will create the IT road map. Components of the solution review can include an executive overview, a business case, a program description, roles and responsibilities, an estimation of program cost, and a risk profile.

- **IT Roadmap Development** – From the solution review, FinCEN will identify new IT and business projects, such as IT development, business process engineering, software investments, and identification of projects that should be charted and managed through the PMO.

- **Identify attainable initiatives for FY 09 budget** – Projects to be funded through the '09 budget must be identified within the next nine months. The re-planning initiative should identify and begin justification and business case activities for those activities.

▫ **Stakeholder Analysis:** This would include an in-depth understanding of the future needs for BSA data and analytics. The preliminary user requirements conducted by FinCEN in 2004 focused more on the current use of data than on future requirements. The stakeholder analysis should include internal analysts, external law enforcement and regulatory users, and agencies that maintain their own copies of BSA data to integrate with other data sets.

5.4 Long-Term Recommendations

Long-term recommendations are those that can be accomplished beyond nine months.

▫ **Establish a Data Quality program:** FinCEN should establish a formal BSA data quality and integrity program. The program should cover the BSA data housed at FinCEN to support complex analytics but also extend to the source files at IRS DCC. The areas to evaluate and improve include: the initial capture of the data on the paper forms and electronic systems, the intake and preprocessing at IRS DCC, the extraction of data files from DCC to FinCEN and other agencies that maintain copies of the BSA data, and the transformation, loading, and management of data in the FinCEN database.

▫ **Own and Control BSA-Related Processes and Resources:** This recommendation was originally made in the Deloitte and Touche 2003 Gap Analysis and continues to be sound. The components of the recommendation include:

- **Establish an oversight role for BSA data processing functions at IRS DCC** - IRS DCC will continue to play a critical role in the collection and processing of BSA data. FinCEN currently lacks a strong oversight role for BSA data processing and should establish greater visibility, a stronger role and a closer relationship with the IRS DCC in this crucial effort.

- **Establish greater influence over BSA Resources** – FinCEN should strive to establish greater control and oversight over all aspects of funding supporting its mission to include funding currently managed by the IRS. This includes developing a formal, joint governance charter with the IRS DCC including performance metrics and service levels for IRS DCC BSA functions.

▫ **BSA Direct R&S Projects:** The re-planning activities conducted in the short-term will determine a roadmap of projects and business initiatives to achieve the BSA Direct R&S vision. These projects should be managed within a BSA Direct R&S program. Assuming the re-planning validates the need for a FinCEN-owned and managed repository of BSA data, the building of this warehouse should be considered as one of the foundation projects.

Acronyms

BI – *Business Intelligence*

BSA – *Bank Secrecy Act*

CBRS – *Currency and Banking Retrieval System, the Internal Revenue Service's data retrieval system*

CCB – *Change Control Board*

CIO – *Chief Information Officer*

CMMI – *Capability Maturity Model® Integration*

COTR – *Contracting Officer's Technical Representative*

COTS – *Commercial Off-the-Shelf*

DCC – *the Internal Revenue Service's Detroit Computing Center*

EA – *Enterprise Architecture*

EAC – *Estimate at Completion*

EDS – *Electronic Data Systems Corporation*

ETL – *Extract, Transform, and Load*

FBI – *Federal Bureau of Investigation*

FinCEN – *Financial Crimes Enforcement Network*

FIU – *Financial Intelligence Unit*

IDS – *Intrusion Detection System*

IDW – *FBI's Investigative Data Warehouse*

IOC – *Initial Operating Capability*

IRS – *Internal Revenue Service*

IT – *Information Technology*

IV&V – *Independent Verification and Validation*

O&M – *Operations and Maintenance*

P.L. – *Public Law*

PM – *Project Manager*

PMO – *Program Management Office*

RFI – *Request for Information*

RFP – *Request for Proposal*

SEI – *Software Engineering Institute*

SOW – *Statement of Work*

UAT – *User Acceptance Testing*

USA PATRIOT Act – *Uniting and Strengthening America by Providing Appropriate Tools Required to Intercept and Obstruct Terrorism*

WebCBRS – *the web-based version of the Internal Revenue Service's Currency and Banking Retrieval System*

www.ingramcontent.com/pod-product-compliance
Lightning Source LLC
Chambersburg PA
CBHW080804290526
45790CB00008B/3581